LOVE LYRICS

SELECTED AND WITH NOTES BY LOUIS UNTERMEYER

ILLUSTRATED BY ANTONIO FRASCONI

THE ODYSSEY PRESS · NEW YORK

"WHAT IS LOVE?"

asks Shakespeare in one of the sweetest songs in *Twelfth Night,* and then proceeds to answer the eternal query:

>   *'Tis not hereafter,*
> *Present mirth hath present laughter.*
>   *What's to come is still unsure;*
> *In delay there lies no plenty.*
> *Then come and kiss me, sweet-and-twenty,*
>   *Youth's a stuff will not endure.*

It is a sentiment that Herrick echoes:

> *Gather ye rosebuds while ye may*
> *Old Time is still a-flying...*

Poets have sung about love endlessly and deathlessly, but nowhere more memorably than in the lyric. Unlike the sonnet, the lyric has no definite shape, no restricted size or measure. As its name suggests, it was once sung to the accompaniment of a lyre. Later the lover wooed his beloved to the strains of a lute or a harp; when the lover could not be his own minstrel, he sent his lady the impassioned verses and let them do the singing for him. But, whatever its form, the lyric was always a spontaneous (and usually brief) outburst of song ■ This is as true today as in the days of the wandering troubadour. The love lyric is a confession, a passionate declaration, a cry from the heart. At one time or another, every poet has expressed it and, in one way or another, every person has repeated it. In spite of its brevity, the power of the love lyric is inexhaustible. It can soar to dazzling heights of ecstasy and drop to bottomless depths of despair; it can attain spiritual rapture as well as the most violent physical stress. "The mind has a thousand eyes, and the heart but one" may sound like a nineteenth century sentimentality (which it was), but it is echoed no less fervently by the twentieth century lover and his lass ■ If love is indefinable—the *Oxford Dictionary of Quotations* lists more than a thousand attempts to define it—the love lyric is immeasurable. This book limits itself to a few of the countless treasures from English-speaking poets. Yet within this limitation there is a remarkably diverse revelation of man's prevalent and sustaining passion, a passion which is both tender and self-torturing, timidly sensitive and outspokenly sensual. Here, in these few pages, the gamut includes the persuasiveness of Shakespeare, the simple directness of Burns, the magic vision of Blake, and the repressed longing of Emily Dickinson ■ We tend to think of lyrics as mere settings for light music. The poets, however, put music into their lines and crystallized the words into pure sound. One of them, Coleridge, summed up the emotional intensity, the exultations and the agonies, in a single definitive stanza:

All thoughts, all passions, all delights,
Whatever stirs this mortal frame,
All are but ministers of Love,
And feed his sacred flame.

William Shakespeare

O mistress mine, where are you roaming?
O stay and hear! your true-love's coming
     That can sing both high and low:
Trip no further, pretty sweeting,
Journeys end in lovers' meeting—
     Every wise man's son doth know.

What is love? 'tis not hereafter;
Present mirth hath present laughter;
     What's to come is still unsure:
In delay there lies no plenty,—
Then come kiss me, Sweet-and-twenty,
     Youth's a stuff will not endure.

Of all the souls that stand create
I have elected one,
When sense from spirit files away
And subterfuge is done;
When that which is and that which was
Apart, intrinsic, stand,
And this brief tragedy of flesh
Is shifted like a sand;

When figures show their royal front
And mists are carved away, -
Behold the atom I preferred
To all the lists of clay!

Emily Dickinson

Good-night? ah! no; the hour is ill
  Which severs those it should unite;
Let us remain together still,
  Then it will be good night.

How can I call the lone night good,
  Though thy sweet wishes wing its flight
Be it not said, thought, understood,
  Then it will be **good** night.

To hearts which near each other move
  From evening close to morning light,
The night is good; because, my love,
  They never say good-night.

Percy Bysshe Shelley

I have been here before,
    But when or how I cannot tell:
I know the grass beyond the door,
    The sweet keen smell,
The sighing sound, the lights around the shore.

        You have been mine before,-
            How long ago I may not know:
        But just when at that swallow's soar
            Your neck turned so,
        Some veil did fall,- I knew it all of yore.

    Has this been thus before?
        And shall not thus time's eddying flight
    Still with our lives our loves restore
        In death's despite,
    And day and night yield one delight once more?

Dante Gabriel Rossetti

Drink to me only with thine eyes,
And I will pledge with mine;
Or leave a kiss but in the cup
And I'll not look for wine.
The thirst that from the soul doth rise
Doth ask a drink divine;
But might I of Jove's nectar sup,
I would not change for thine.

Ben Jonson

I sent thee late a rosy wreath,
Not so much honouring thee
As giving it a hope that there
It could not withered be;
But thou thereon didst only breathe
And sent'st it back to me;
Since when it grows, and smells, I swear,
Not of itself but thee!

Over the mountains
And over the waves;
Under the fountains,
And under the graves;
Under floods that are deepest,
Which Neptune obey;
Over rocks that are steepest,
Love will find out the way.

You may train the eagle
To stoop to your fist;
Or you may inveigle
The phoenix of the east;
The lioness, ye may move her
To give o'er her prey;
But you'll ne'er stop a lover:
He will find out his way.

Love me not for comely grace,
    For my pleasing eye or face,
Not for any outward part,
No, nor for a constant heart:
    For these may fail or turn to ill,
    So thou and I shall sever:
Keep, therefore, a true woman's eye,
And love me still but know not why—
    So hast thou the same reason still
    To dote upon me ever!

Author unknown

Robert Louis Stevenson

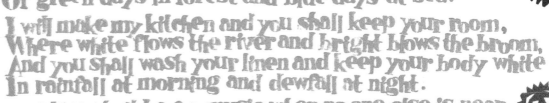

I will make you brooches and toys for your delight
Of bird-song at morning and star-shine at night.
I will make a palace fit for you and me
Of green days in forest and blue days at sea.

I will make my kitchen and you shall keep your room,
Where white flows the river and bright blows the broom,
And you shall wash your linen and keep your body white
In rainfall at morning and dewfall at night.

And this shall be for music when no one else is near,
The fine song for singing, the rare song to hear!
That only I remember, that only you admire,
Of the broad road that stretches and the roadside fire.

My heart is like a singing bird
Whose nest is in a water'd shoot;
My heart is like an apple-tree
Whose boughs are bent with thick-set fruit;
My heart is like a rainbow shell
That paddles in a halcyon sea;
My heart is gladder than all these,
Because my love is come to me.

Raise me a dais of silk and down;
Hang it with vair and purple dyes;
Carve it in doves and pomegranates,
And peacocks with a hundred eyes;
Work it in gold and silver grapes,
In leaves and silver fleurs-de-lys;
Because the birthday of my life
Is come, my love is come to me.

Christina Georgina Rossetti

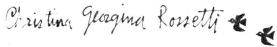

She walks in beauty, like the night
    Of cloudless climes and starry skies;
And all that's best of dark and bright
    Meet in her aspect and her eyes:
Thus mellow'd to that tender light
    Which heaven to gaudy day denies.

One shade the more, one ray the less,
    Had half impair'd the nameless grace
Which waves in every raven tress,
    Or softly lightens o'er her face;
Where thoughts serenely sweet express
    How pure, how dear their dwelling-place.

And on that cheek, and o'er that brow,
    So soft, so calm, yet eloquent,
The smiles that win, the tints that glow,
    But tell of days in goodness spent,
A mind at peace with all below,
    A heart whose love is innocent!

George Gordon,
Lord Byron

O my Luve is like a red, red rose,
  That's newly sprung in June:
O my Luve is like the melodie,
  That's sweetly played in tune.

As fair art thou, my bonie lass,
  So deep in luve am I
And I will luve thee still, my dear,
  Till a' the seas gang dry.

Till a' the seas gang dry, my dear,
    And the rocks melt wi' the sun;
And I will luve thee still, my dear,
    While the sands o' life shall run.

And fare-thee-weel, my only Luve!
    And fare-thee-weel a while!
And I will come again, my Luve,
    Tho' it were ten thousand mile.

Robert Burns

My feet are winged, while o'er the dewy lawn
I meet my maiden risen like the morn.
Oh, bless those holy feet, like angel's feet;
Oh, bless those limbs, beaming with heavenly light.

Like as an angel glittering in the sky
In times of innocence and holy joy;
The joyful shepherd stops his grateful song
To hear the music of an angel's tongue.

So, when she speaks, the voice of Heaven I hear;
So, when we walk, nothing impure comes near;
Each field seems Eden, and each calm retreat,
Each village seems the haunt of holy feet.

William Blake

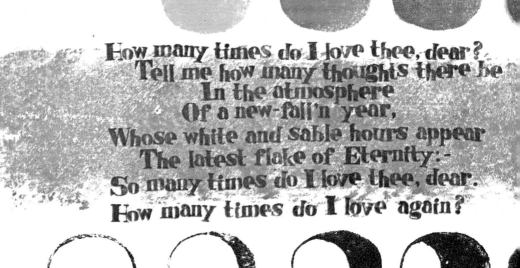

How many times do I love thee, dear?
Tell me how many thoughts there be
In the atmosphere
Of a new-fall'n year,
Whose white and sable hours appear
The latest flake of Eternity:—
So many times do I love thee, dear.
How many times do I love again?

Tell me how many beads there are
In a silver chain
Of evening rain,
Unravelled from the tumbling main,
And threading the eye of a yellow star:-
So many times do I love again.

Thomas Lovell Beddoes

A. E. Housman

When I was one-and-twen
I heard a wise man say

Give crowns and pounds and guineas
      But not your heart away;
Give pearls away and rubies
      But keep your fancy free."
But I was one-and-twenty,
      No use to talk to me.
            When I was one-and-twenty
                  I heard him say again,
            "The heart out of the bosom
                  Was never given in vain;
            'Tis paid with sighs a-plenty
                  And sold for endless rue."
            And I am two-and-twenty,
                  And oh, 'tis true, 'tis true.

Now sleeps the crimson petal, now the white
Nor waves the cypress in the palace walk;
Nor winks the gold fin in the porphyry font:
The firefly wakens: waken thou with me.

Now droops the milkwhite peacock like a gho
And like a ghost she glimmers on to me.

Now lies the Earth all Danaë to the stars
And all thy heart lies open unto me.

Now slides the silent meteor on, and leaves
A shining furrow, as thy thoughts in me.

Now folds the lily all her sweetness up,
And slips into the bosom of the lake;
So fold thyself, my dearest, thou, and slip
Into my bosom and be lost in me.

Alfred, Lord Tennyson

The moth's kiss, first!
Kiss me as if you made me believe
You were not sure, this eve,
How my face, your flower, had pursed
Its petals up; so, here and there
You brush it, till I grow aware
Who wants me, and wide open I burst.

The bee's kiss, now!
Kiss me as if you enter'd gay
My heart at some noonday,
A bud that dares not disallow
The claim, so all is render'd up,
And passively its shatter'd cup
Over your head to sleep I bow.

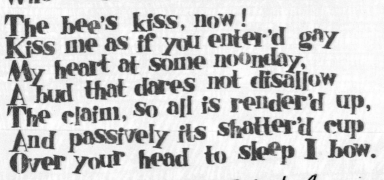

Robert Browning

The nightingale has a lyre of gold,
  The lark's is a clarion call,
And the blackbird plays but a boxwood flute
  But I love him best of all.

For his song is all of the joy of life,
And we in the mad spring weather,
We too have listened till he sang
Our hearts and lips together.

William Ernest Henley

Only of thee and me the nightwind sings:
  Only of us the lovers speak at sea;
The earth is full of breathless whisperings
  Only of thee and me.

Only of thee and me the forests chant;
    Only of us the stir in bush and tree;
The rain and sun inform the blossoming plant
    Only of thee and me.

Only of thee and me till all shall fade;
    Only of us the world's first thought can be;
For we are love, and heaven itself is made
    Only of thee and me.

Louis Untermeyer

WILLIAM SHAKESPEARE (1564–1616) did not write some of the world's loveliest lyrics as individual poems to stand by themselves. The songs interspersed throughout his plays were written for the theatre as theatrical expedients. Their purpose was to prepare a mood, sustain a situation, herald an entrance with flourish or end a scene with a final cadence. Nevertheless, by themselves the songs are perfect lyrics. If Shakespeare had written nothing else, a glorious reputation could rest on these.

■ BEN JONSON (1572–1637), Shakespeare's great friend, possessed a lyric genius almost as great as Shakespeare's. In youth he worked as a bricklayer; in his twenties he wrote a comedy in which Shakespeare acted; in his thirties and early forties he composed a variety of plays ranging from tragedies to satires, pageants and masques; in his mid-forties he was appointed England's first poet laureate. He was buried in Westminster Abbey, and an inscription on his tomb shows the regard in which he was held. It reads: "O Rare Ben Jonson."

■ WILLIAM BLAKE (1757–1827) believed that his writings, engravings, and the mystical designs which frame his poems were inspired by communications from the invisible world, the world of the spirit. When he was eight he beheld a tree filled with angels; years later he said that heaven pressed so close he could touch it with his walking stick. His imaginative power was inimitable and his range tremendous, from the childlike *Songs of Innocence* to the prophetical *Marriage of Heaven and Hell*. Even if unsigned, everything Blake created, even the simplest songs, bears his unmistakable signature.

■ ROBERT BURNS (1759–1796) was not the "heaven-taught plowman" which his worshipers delight to glorify. He was a woefully unsuccessful farmer who carefully studied the elements of the poetic craft, published a collection of poems at twenty-seven, became a celebrity, a season's sensation, displeased the hierarchy, turned radical, grew ill, and died wretchedly. His "affairs" were as notorious as they were numerous. But his devotion to Jean Armour, whom he eventually married, was touching and his artless love songs have a beauty and vitality which make them outlive far more elegant performances.

■ GEORGE GORDON, LORD BYRON (1788–1824) was the son of an irresponsible libertine; he outdid his father in continuous and sometimes eccentric amours. As a poet he was both facile and forceful; he published *Childe Harold's Pilgrimage* at twenty-four and woke one morning to find himself famous. Byron's chief subject was a glamorized version of himself; he was always his own hero. His life was a long, feverish romance, and his death was romantic in the heroic tradition. He died in an attempt to liberate Greece from Turkish tyranny.

■ PERCY BYSSHE SHELLEY (1792–1822) lived a short life of revolt against the conventions. Expelled from college at eighteen for writing a pamphlet, *The Necessity of Atheism,* he defended his attitude by saying "Language is given us to express ideas—he who fetters it is a tyrant." At nineteen he eloped with Harriet Westbrook, who was little more than fifteen, and, after three years, left her for Mary Godwin, daughter of the anarchical William Godwin. Shelley's tenets of free and platonic love mingle with a passion for liberty in some of the most unrestrained lyrics ever written. Living breathlessly, he died, drowned, at thirty.

■ THOMAS LOVELL BEDDOES (1803–1849) began life as a prodigy and ended it as an insane suicide. Before he was seventeen he had won two important prizes (one for Latin, one for Greek), had published poems, and had finished a play. Nothing has survived except a few songs from his unactable dramas, but the songs themselves are exquisite.

■ ALFRED, LORD TENNYSON (1809–1892), unlike most poets, lived in comfort accompanied by fame and attended by homage. The homage came not only from a multitude of worshipful commoners but also from Queen Victoria. This was appropriate as well as logical, for the poetry of Tennyson epitomized the Victorian era. His *In Memoriam* won him the laureateship; *Idylls of the King* brought him the reward of a peerage. Once the most widely read poet of the period, Tennyson has receded in popular esteem, but he is due for a revival. A recent selection of his work was introduced with an illuminating introduction by W. H. Auden. Not even the most critical commentator can doubt that Tennyson's best lyrics are imperishable.

■ ROBERT BROWNING (1812–1889) presents a double paradox. The most erudite of poets, he never attended a university; the most skillful delineator of psychological portraits, he gave romantic subjects vivid reality and enlivened classicism with an almost jaunty technique. His union with Elizabeth Barrett, an invalid six years his senior and, at the time of their marriage, a more popular poet than he, became one of the great love stories in literature as well as life.

■ DANTE GABRIEL ROSSETTI (1828–1882) was a self-contradiction as a poet and a painter. A pagan at heart, he was preoccupied with religious subjects and sentiments. His most famous poem, *The Blessed Damozel,* and the painting he made of it, visualize the longing of a lover and mystic. The strange langour and subdued sensuality of Rossetti's was considered "sacrilegious," and the Pre-Raphaelite Brotherhood which he helped found was attacked as "The Fleshly School of Poetry."

■ CHRISTINA ROSSETTI (1830–1894) was far more undeviating in her religious affiliations than her brother, Dante Gabriel. A devout Anglican, she denied herself the love of two men; refusing marriage, she considered herself bound to a heavenly bridegroom. A recluse, she wrote voluminously; her *Collected Poems* contain almost a thousand hymns, sonnets, and lyrics, many of which are rapt and exalted.

■ EMILY DICKINSON (1830–1886) shunned the world

even more severely than Christina Rossetti. Although she wrote close to 1800 poems, she wrote them in secret; she never offered anything to be printed. "Publication is the auction of the mind," she declared. Because of an unconsummated love, at twenty-four she secluded herself in her home in Amherst, composing and putting away the most dazzling poetry ever conceived and perfected by a woman.

■ WILLIAM ERNEST HENLEY (1849–1903) suffered as a child from tuberculosis; a foot had to be amputated. Possibly because of his continued poor health, he celebrated strength and energy. Triumphing over his handicaps, Henley became an editor, critic, playwright and, first and last, a poet. Best known for *Invictus,* Henley wrote many lyrics that vibrate with impassioned sincerity.

■ ROBERT LOUIS STEVENSON (1850–1894) was, like his good friend, W. E. Henley, afflicted with tuberculosis. He tried to escape the disease in various parts of the world; it finally killed him in Samoa. Primarily a writer of adventure stories *(Treasure Island* and *Kidnapped),* he is also childhood's laureate *(A Child's Garden of Verses)* and (as in the lyric included here) the lover's romancer.

■ ALFRED EDWARD HOUSMAN (1859–1936) was universally acclaimed for *A Shropshire Lad* in 1896; almost a quarter of a century passed before Housman issued his next volume, which he significantly called *Last Poems.* Retreating from the modern world, Housman immured himself in classicism—he devoted twenty-seven years to a study of Manilius, a minor Latin poet. His own compact poems are tinctured with a sometimes blithe and sometimes bitter irony.

■ LOUIS UNTERMEYER (1885–   ) is the author, editor, and compiler of some ninety volumes of prose and poetry, including this one.